The Government's Expenditure Plans, 1978-79 to 1981-82

Volume I

Presented to Parliament by the Chancellor of the Exchequer
by Command of Her Majesty
January 1978

LONDON
HER MAJESTY'S STATIONERY OFFICE
70p net

Cmnd 7049—I

ISBN 0 10 170490 9

THE GOVERNMENT'S EXPENDITURE PLANS, 1978–79 TO 1981–82

PART I

Contents   *Paragraph No.*

SUMMARY OF TABLES

THE GOVERNMENT'S EXPENDITURE PLANS, 1978–79 TO 1981–82

PART 1

This White Paper presents the Government's latest plans for public expenditure. Volume I gives a general account of the plans and their economic and fiscal context, Volume II details of individual expenditure programmes and supporting material.

2. The improvement in the country's financial situation, to which the cuts in public expenditure plans which preceded last year's White Paper (Cmnd 6721) made an important contribution, enables the Government now to plan for resumed and continuing expansion of many programmes financed by public expenditure. Along with other measures to improve the outlook for employment and to bring the growth of output on to its intended path, the Chancellor of the Exchequer announced on 26 October 1977 the Government's decision to add £1 billion[1] to the plans for 1978–79. That decision is reflected in the present White Paper.

3. Renewed expansion in expenditure plans must be governed by the Government's broad economic objectives of containing inflation, reducing unemployment and promoting industrial efficiency. In addition, the Government now aim at a greater degree of stability than has been achieved in recent years, so that expenditure programmes can be managed with confidence that they will not be subjected to the disruption of sudden cuts.

4. Both for this reason, and in order to leave room for manoeuvre on taxation, it is necessary that the planned growth rate for total public expenditure should be within the prospective growth rate of national income. The present plans are constituted to this end. As always those for the later years are provisional. The Government want to improve and in many cases expand the provision of public services, and will do so as circumstances permit; but they do not intend to set up plans which go beyond what the economy can safely be assumed capable of sustaining.

5. The Government intend to maintain and develop the procedures of expenditure control, including the new features introduced in recent years, such as the system of cash limits and strict observance of the announced control figure for the contingency reserve, and the arrangements for monitoring expenditure in the course of the year as described in Cmnd 6721. The latter is an important management tool which, as experience grows in its use, should promote a closer match between plans and outturn.

---

[1] All figures in this White Paper are at 1977 survey prices unless otherwise stated. They have been rounded and do not therefore necessarily sum to the totals.

Summary of the plans

6. The planning figures for public expenditure until 1981–82 are shown in table 1, together with the Cmnd 6721 planning figures for the current year. The tables at the end of this volume give more details.

Public expenditure plans

TABLE 1

£ million at 1977 survey prices

	1977–78 as in Cmnd 6721	1978–79	1979–80	1980–81	1981–82
Expenditure on programmes:					
Central government	39,572	41,655	41,980	42,418	42,570
Local authorities	15,407	15,493	15,719	15,890	15,992
Total general government	54,979	57,148	57,699	58,308	58,562
Certain public corporations(¹)	993	952	1,012	1,002	1,015
Total expenditure on programmes	55,972	58,100	58,711	59,310	59,577
Contingency reserve	750	750	1,500	1,750	2,000
Total	56,722	58,850	60,211	61,060	61,577
Debt interest	2,500	2,000	1,900	1,800	1,600
Total public expenditure	59,222	60,850	62,111	62,860	63,177
Total programmes, contingency reserve and net overseas and market borrowing of nationalised industries	57,267	58,550	59,611	60,860	61,327

(¹) Corporations whose capital expenditure is included in public expenditure; mainly the water authorities, the housing corporation and the new town development corporations. These corporations do not include the nationalised industries. A list is given in part 6.

7. The figures for the year immediately ahead, 1978–79, are firm plans. These provide the basis of Estimates, cash limits and rate support grant. The figures for the succeeding years are increasingly provisional: they will be reviewed in successive annual surveys.

8. The planned total of public expenditure programmes and the contingency reserve for 1978–79, adjusted to include the total net borrowing requirement of the nationalised industries (see paragraph 9 below), is approximately £1 billion higher, at 1977 survey prices, than the provisional plans for that year published in Cmnd 6721.

9. Public expenditure, as defined in these White Papers, includes finance provided by the Government to the nationalised industries, whether by loans, public dividend capital or grants. The amount provided by the Government is greatly affected by the net amounts which the industries borrow from, or repay to, overseas lenders or the market. As the Select Committee on

Expenditure have pointed out, such borrowing, or repayments, can distort the year-to-year path of government lending to the industries, and hence of public expenditure as a whole: over the next few years the industries are due to repay substantial amounts borrowed from overseas lenders in the mid-1970s, and to replace this by borrowing from the National Loans Fund. One way of discounting this is to adjust the planned total of programmes and the contingency reserve to include the *total* net borrowing requirement of the nationalised industries (not just what the Government lends to them). The last line of table 1 gives figures for the total adjusted in this way([1]).

10. This adjusted total rises by about 2¼ per cent in 1978–79, compared with the Cmnd 6721 plans for the current year (1977–78)([2]). The rate of growth in the two succeeding years—1979–80 and 1980–81—is of the order of 2 per cent a year. The present figure for 1981–82 is under 1 per cent, but the plans in the later years are increasingly provisional and subject to revision in subsequent surveys; this applies especially to the final year. The precise figures are:

1978–79	1979–80	1980–81	1981–82
+2.2%	+1.8%	+2.1%	+0.8%

Expenditure in 1976–77

11. At outturn prices, total public expenditure in 1976–77 was £55¼ billion. This was nearly 11 per cent more than the outturn price figure for 1975–76, but in volume terms (constant prices) the total of programmes excluding debt interest was *less* than in 1975–76, by nearly 3½ per cent. This fall owed much to a reduction in net government lending to nationalised industries, as the industries borrowed heavily in foreign currency. In total public expenditure including debt interest the fall was somewhat less than in programmes alone, because payments of debt interest increased. Table 2 gives the figures.

12. The outturn of programmes in 1976–77 was less in volume terms than the Cmnd 6721 plans for that year, by about 3¾ per cent, or £2¼ billion at 1977 survey prices.

13. One major difference between plans and outturn was in programme 5, government lending to nationalised industries. This is a particularly difficult programme to forecast. The 1976–77 outturn figure of £330 million was not only much lower than in the previous year (see paragraph 11 above) but also well below the 1976–77 provision of £917 million in Cmnd 6721: overseas borrowing by the industries was greater than assumed in Cmnd 6721, which provided only for such overseas borrowing as had already been undertaken when the figures were prepared. In addition, both the trading results and the capital expenditure of the nationalised industries turned out differently from the assumptions used in Cmnd 6721.

([1]) For changes in this adjusted total since Cmnd 6721, see table 14, row M.

([2]) The increase compared with the latest estimates for 1977–78 is much greater, but this is not a valid comparison: the latest estimates for 1977–78 provide for some underspending but no such provision is made in the plans for 1978–79, although under-spending is likely to occur in that year also. See further paragraphs 21–22.

14. The aggregate outturn in 1976–77 in volume terms on all programmes other than the nationalised industries was about 3 per cent below the planning figure in Cmnd 6721. In some programmes, notably education, health and social security, the difference was slight, but outturn was below the plan in every programme. Details are in tables 13 and 15 and in Part 2.

15. Many factors contributed to this difference. The more extensive use of cash limits was itself probably one, as many programme managers were especially careful to run no risk of exceeding their limits. On the central government programmes covered by cash limits, expenditure (at outturn prices) was about 2 per cent or £600 million below those limits. In volume terms the difference was somewhat greater, since prices rose faster than had been allowed for when the cash limits were set. Another factor was that expenditure on new measures to promote employment turned out less than the original estimate. Other factors included over-provision for refinance of export credit, unavoidable delays in obtaining some defence equipment, and delays in road building as a result of weather conditions in the second half of the year.

16. The volume of local authority current expenditure was marginally below that envisaged just before the year began for England and Wales, and marginally above for Scotland. The overrun expected last autumn, and built into the Cmnd 6721 figures, did not occur.

Public expenditure 1974–75 to 1977–78

TABLE 2

£ million at 1977 survey prices

	1974–75	1975–76	1976–77	1977–78 estimated
Expenditure on programmes:				
Central government	39,661	40,279	39,238	38,233
Local authorities	16,931	16,846	15,916	15,165
Total general government	56,592	57,125	55,154	53,398
Certain public corporations(¹)	1,138	1,176	1,047	922
Total expenditure on programmes ...	57,729	58,301	56,201	54,320
Debt interest	907	1,169	1,662	1,900
Total public expenditure	58,636	59,470	57,863	56,220
Total programmes and net overseas and market borrowing of nationalised industries	58,742	59,077	57,635	54,739

(¹) See note (¹) to table 1.

Expenditure in 1977–78

17. Table 2 summarises the estimate of outturn in 1977–78 used in this White Paper, alongside the latest estimates for the past three years. For 1977–78 the volume of expenditure on programmes is now put at about 95½ per cent

4

of the Cmnd 6721 provision for programmes and contingency reserve. In addition, the expected net outturn of debt interest is significantly below the figures in Cmnd 6721.

18.   A considerable part of the difference of 4½ per cent between the outturn for programmes now expected and the earlier plans is attributable to two major items: government lending to nationalised industries, which is again expected to be substantially lower than planned initially, and refinancing of export and shipbuilding credit, which, partly owing to the new arrangements with the banks, is expected to show net repayments to the government this year. Apart from these two items, the outturn is now estimated at over 97 per cent of the Cmnd 6721 plans.

19.   The changes from Cmnd 6721 reflect many causes. For example, lower interest rates have reduced the scale of housing subsidies, some delay is still being experienced in defence works and procurement programmes and, in some cases, firmer estimates of expenditure in 1976–77 have led to revised estimates for the current year.

20.   The value of central government expenditure covered by cash limits in the first half of the financial year was about 3¼ per cent below what departments had expected at the beginning of the year. For the year as a whole the estimates given in this White Paper reflect the belief of departments that the volume of their expenditure over the full year will be somewhat nearer the initial plans. For local authority current expenditure the figures now given are consistent with those available at the time of the negotiation of the rate support grant for 1978–79.

21.   Some continuing divergence between planning figures and outturn is to be expected in future years. Any system of control which applies limits to programmes will normally result in outturns being somewhat less than planned levels. The likelihood of such shortfall is taken into account in the forecasts for the economy and the public sector borrowing requirement which inform the Government's consideration of public expenditure, and hence in the decisions on the planned level of expenditure.([1])

22.   How completely plans will be achieved in any one year is hard to predict, particularly in the light of recent experience. There is a general tendency to over-estimate the extent to which expenditure can be increased rapidly in the short run. But increasing familiarity with the new control and information systems should promote a closer match between estimates and outturn.

Expenditure plans, 1978–79 and after

Central government

23.   The main services provided by the central government (including transfer payments) account for over 70 per cent of total programmes. Figures for these services are summarised in table 3.

---

[1] An allowance for shortfall is made below in the table 8 projections of expenditure and revenue.

Central government expenditure programmes
TABLE 3

£ million at 1977 survey prices

	1975–76	1976–77	1977–78 estimated	1978–79	1979–80
Defence	6,445	6,361	6,255	6,289	6,494
National health service	5,981	6,051	6,132	6,255	6,350
Social security	12,309	12,717	13,226	14,063	14,172
Other expenditure	15,544	14,109	12,620	15,048	14,964
Total	40,279	39,238	38,233	41,655	41,980

24. About 40 per cent of public expenditure by the central government, excluding debt interest, is on goods and services, the largest elements being defence and the national health service. The remainder consists of transfer payments—including social security benefits, housing subsidies and industrial support—and net lending, which includes loans to nationalised industries.

Nationalised industries

25. The table 3 figures for public expenditure by the central government include provision for government lending to the nationalised industries. Estimates of this lending are shown in table 4, along with estimates of the total net borrowing requirement of the industries, which are included in the adjusted planning total in table 1. The differences between the two sets of figures reflect the industries' net borrowing from, or repayments to, the market and overseas, and in particular the major programme of foreign currency and market debt repayments which the industries are expected to make between 1978–79 and 1980–81. The precise timing of this programme is uncertain. If repayments were made sooner than assumed in table 4, that would affect the figures for net government lending, but total net borrowing by the industries would not be affected to any great extent.

Nationalised industries' borrowing
TABLE 4

£ million at 1977 survey prices

	1976–77	1977–78 estimated	1978–79	1979–80	1980–81	1981–82
Net government lending	330	420	1,350	1,550	1,350	1,100
Total net borrowing (other than short-term)	1,764	950	1,050	950	1,150	850

26. The estimates for total net borrowing show the industries' requirements for loans from all sources and for public dividend capital. They depend on assumptions about the level of investment by the industries, their markets, pricing policies and productivity. They may need to be revised further when the Government has completed the process of setting financial targets for each of the industries, and in the light of the current consideration of the problems of the British Steel Corporation.

27. Notwithstanding these uncertainties, the fall in the industries' overal lent borrowing requirement after 1976–77 marks an improvement in the financial position of most of them. After the deficits caused by price restraint in the early 1970s most of the industries are now profitable again as a result of the progressive return to economic pricing. They are therefore able to make a substantial contribution to the financing of their own investment which is expected to amount to about £3½ billion in 1977–78 and in 1978–79. It is part of the Government's medium term expenditure strategy that this improvement in the industries' financial position should be maintained.

28. Volume II contains a commentary on each of the nationalised industry programmes and presents figures for the industries' capital investment programmes and their financing.

Local authorities

29. Local authorities are responsible for more than one-quarter of public expenditure. They are responsible for the greater part of expenditure on education (which accounts for more than half of their current expenditure), on housing (which accounts for a similar proportion of their capital spending), and on other environmental services. They employ more than one in ten of the working population.

30. The Government does not have the same direct control over expenditure by local authorities as over its own spending. Part 1 of Cmnd 6721 explained the means of influence open to the Government and the extent to which the Government's ability to regulate this expenditure within a reasonable margin is dependent on the co-operation of local government. Green Papers on Local Government Finance (Cmnd 6811 and 6813) were published in May 1977 following the report of the Layfield Committee. These emphasised the need to develop, on a partnership basis between central and local government, the duties and responsibilities involved in the provision of local public services. They proposed financial arrangements designed to give a substantial degree of local autonomy while safeguarding the central government's economic responsibilities and policy interests. This was intended to provide a satisfactory long-term basis for ensuring that total local authority expenditure was maintained at a level which the country can afford. Discussions are continuing with the local authority associations about these proposals.

31. Over the past three years, current expenditure by local authorities has had to be reined back. A year ago it was still feared that the adjustment was not being achieved as quickly as the Government had hoped, and that an absolute reduction in the volume of expenditure might be required in 1978–79. In the event, a rate of growth which had reached nearly 10 per cent in the one year 1974–75 has been succeeded by an increase of only about half that amount over the whole of the following three-year period.

32. General recognition of the requirements of the economic situation, and restrictions on the availability of government finance, have no doubt contributed to the speed with which this necessary adjustment has been achieved. But it also illustrates the increasingly close co-operation between central and

7

local government in the planning and control of public expenditure, through the Consultative Councils on Local Government Finance in England and Wales and in discussions with the Convention of Scottish Local Authorities.

Public expenditure by local authorities (Great Britain)

TABLE 5

£ million at 1977 survey prices

	1975–76	1976–77	1977–78 estimated	1978–79	1979–80
Current expenditure:					
Environmental services(¹)	1,489	1,432	1,467	1,446	1,484
Law, order and protective services ...	1,321	1,378	1,393	1,416	1,432
Education and libraries, science and					
arts	6,351	6,384	6,438	6,535	6,568
Health and personal social services	987	1,012	1,044	1,072	1,096
Other programmes	1,663	1,540	1,500	1,494	1,512
Total	11,811	11,746	11,843	11,962	12,092
Capital expenditure	4,817	3,951	3,088	3,287	3,377
Total	16,628	15,697	14,930	15,249	15,469

¹ Programme 8 "other environmental services"

33. It is no longer necessary for the total volume of current expenditure to be cut in 1978–79. After taking account of demographic factors and of the continuing revenue effects of capital projects, there will be little scope for improvements in the level of service provision, and continued restraint in local authority spending plans will be necessary. However, as the figures in table 5 show, the rate support grant settlements for 1978–79 provide for some resumption of growth in the total of current expenditure.

34. Similarly, the plans in Cmnd 6721 for the capital expenditure of local authorities also provided for a reduction in 1978–79 compared with the current year. Now it is possible to look ahead to a small increase. The figures shown in table 5 reflect the special measures to assist the construction industry announced during 1977.

35. The Government will be discussing the implications of the plans in this White Paper for the years after 1978–79 with the local authority associations in the Consultative Councils and the Convention in the normal course of the next public expenditure survey.

36. The definition of local authority current expenditure for White Paper purposes differs in certain respects from "relevant expenditure" which is the aggregate on which the level of government grants to local authorities is based each year following the rate support grant discussions. For 1978–79 the percentage of aggregate Exchequer grant has been fixed at the same level as for 1977–78, that is 61 per cent for England and Wales and 68½ per cent for Scotland. Table 6 shows how relevant expenditure has been financed since 1975–76 as between central and local sources of revenue and how the Government expects it will be financed next year. A reconciliation between local authority current expenditure in public expenditure survey terms and "relevant expenditure" is given in Volume II of this White Paper.

8

Financing of local authority relevant expenditure (Great Britain)([1])

TABLE 6

£ million at outturn prices

	1975–76	1976–77	1977–78 estimated	1978–79
Total expenditure([2])	11,240	12,630	13,950	15,120
Financed by:				
Government grants	7,420	8,260	8,590	9,280
Local rates and rate rebate grants	4,340	4,680	5,350	} 5,840
Drawings from (+)/additions to (−) local balances etc	− 520	− 310	10	

[1] Excludes VAT paid by local authorities.
[2] Includes a small element of expenditure met from rates which is not relevant for grant purposes.

Contingency reserve

37. The planning totals for the years ahead include substantial contingency reserves to cover unforeseen items and items which cannot be properly quantified at this stage. The scale of provision is shown in table 1, line 6. The size of the contingency reserve for the later years is reviewed along with the spending programmes in each successive annual survey.

38. As explained in Cmnd 6721, any addition to a programme decided upon during the year is charged against the contingency reserve if it cannot be offset by an appropriate saving in the programme concerned or other programmes. The arrangements for approving claims on the contingency reserve, and for monitoring these claims, form an important part of the Government's procedures for control of public expenditure.

Debt interest

39. The figures for total public expenditure shown in table 1 include debt interest, but debt interest payments are not included in the planning totals discussed in paragraphs 7–10 above. In Cmnd 6721 a new concept of debt interest payments was introduced, including only those payments which have to be financed from taxation or further government borrowing. Payments met from interest receipts on money lent, or for which provision is made from trading surpluses or rents, are excluded.

40. On this basis the estimate for 1977–78 is £1,900 million compared with the 1976–77 figure of £1,662 million (both at 1977 survey prices). The estimates for this year and next are substantially below those in Cmnd 6721, which were £2,500 million and £1,760 million respectively, on a comparable basis. The reductions are due mainly to lower borrowing and interest rates than were assumed when the Cmnd 6721 estimates were made. Volume II of this White Paper gives a fuller explanation.

Analysis by economic category

41. Tables 10 and 12 show that the economic analysis of public expenditure is not expected to change much over the planning period. Current expenditure on goods and services, which now accounts for nearly half the total, continues to rise slowly.

42. Public expenditure on fixed investment increases over the planning period but remains relatively low compared with the years up to 1975–76. Most of it is construction work, and the extra spending on construction announced during 1977 means that a steady level of direct public spending on construction in the next four years is now planned, at about £4½ billion a year. In addition, government grants and lending help to finance other construction work, for example by the nationalised industries and housing associations. If construction expenditure by those bodies is included, the total planned level of public spending on construction rises to some £6¼ billion in 1978–79 and continues at a similar level through to 1981–82. Fuller details are being published separately and will appear in the next issue of "Housing and Construction Statistics".

43. Transfer payments increase in total over the planning period, with some changes in composition. Payments to individuals, notably of pensions and other social security benefits, continue to rise, while subsidies tend to fall. There are marked changes in net lending, including the increased government lending to nationalised industries and the reduced government refinancing of fixed rate export and shipbuilding credit mentioned earlier.

Public expenditure and gross domestic product (GDP)

44. In the first half of this decade public expenditure continued to grow at much the same rate as in the previous decade, while national disposable income grew very little, partly because of the slow growth in output and partly because of the deterioration in the terms of trade. The ratio of total public expenditure to GDP[1] increased from 38 per cent in 1971–72 to 46 per cent in 1975–76, and fell to 44½ per cent in 1976–77.

45. This ratio is not a wholly satisfactory indicator of the importance of the public sector in the economy as a whole. Total public expenditure includes transfers and loans to the private sector, which require government taxation or borrowing but finance private, not public, consumption and investment. Moreover, the total is affected by changes in the extent to which the nationalised industries rely on the Government to meet their external financing needs.

46. For some purposes a more useful ratio is that for general government[2] expenditure on goods and services. This ratio rose from 22½ per cent of GDP in 1971–72 to 27 per cent in 1975–76, and fell to 26 per cent in 1976–77. On either basis there was a sharp increase up to 1975–76 followed by some fall last year. Table 7 gives a run of figures.

---

[1] To calculate these ratios total public expenditure is taken at current prices (or, for future years, in cost terms) and increased by an estimate of the value of government capital assets consumed during the year to make the figures comparable with the figures of GDP. The latter are measured at market prices (inclusive of indirect taxes and net subsidies) because this is the valuation basis of the public expenditure figures. The provision for capital consumption was included in the figures for government consumption and GDP this year for the first time in place of the former concept of notional or imputed rent on buildings owned and occupied by the Government.

[2] Central government and local authorities.

10

Ratios of public expenditure to GDP at market prices

TABLE 7per cent

						Total public expenditure	General government expenditure on goods and services
1971–72 ...	...	...	...	...	...	38	22½
1972–73 ...	...	...	...	...	...	39	22½
1973–74 ...	...	...	...	...	...	41	24
1974–75 ...	...	...	...	...	...	45½	26
1975–76 ...	...	...	...	...	...	46	27
1976–77 ...	...	...	...	...	...	44½	26

47.   On present expenditure plans and the illustrative assumptions on GDP growth made in paragraph 58, the ratios for subsequent years would be lower than in 1976–77; but the growth of transfer payments in the total is likely to keep the ratio of total public expenditure to GDP well above what it was in the early 1970s.

The economic and fiscal context

48.   In all industrialised countries the period since the oil price increases in late 1973 has been marked by high levels of unemployment and by rates of inflation which have remained high by previous standards. The persistence of inflation and, in many cases, the external financing problems created by the oil producers' surpluses have inhibited actions by governments to stimulate activity. Except in the United States, recovery from the recession has been hesitant and insufficient to stem the tide of rising unemployment. World trade has been depressed.

49.   Between 1973 and 1977 there was no change in output in the United Kingdom; and real national disposable income fell by 2¼ per cent, reflecting the adverse movement in the terms of trade. Whereas public and personal consumption had been growing more or less in line over the previous decade, they diverged after 1973: personal consumption actually fell between 1973 and 1977 while public authorities' consumption rose at an average annual rate of 2½ per cent. The fall in real take-home pay was even sharper than the fall in personal consumption, which was moderated by substantial increases in social security benefits. Investment, public and private, fell during the period. But there was a substantial improvement in the balance of payments.

50.   Considerable progress was made in 1977 in carrying through the adaptation of the UK economy, and in particular in removing the financial imbalances that had proved so disruptive in 1976. The current account of the balance of payments moved into surplus, helped by the increasing flow of North Sea oil and an improvement in the terms of trade but also by a strong rise in the volume of exports. The rate of inflation decelerated. Confidence returned to the financial markets and was reflected both in lower interest rates and the strength of sterling.

51. In contrast to the financial indicators the real economy was sluggish. It became both feasible and desirable to give a stimulus to activity. In October the Chancellor of the Exchequer announced measures estimated to raise the rate of growth by about 1 per cent in 1978, to $3\frac{1}{2}$ per cent. He emphasised that attainment of this faster growth rate would depend on an average earnings rise in the current pay round consistent with the Government's guidelines: that is, not more than 10 per cent. Any faster rise in earnings would reduce growth by its adverse effects on confidence, interest rates and competitiveness.

52. The uncertainty over the future rate of inflation poses the major question mark over the medium-term prospects for the economy. A second uncertainty, partly linked with inflation, concerns the growth of productivity, and hence of the economy's productive potential. Over the 25 years or so up to the beginning of the recent recession the trend rate of growth of gross domestic product was $2\frac{3}{4}$ per cent a year. Over the past four years output has been virtually flat, and there has been almost no growth in recorded productivity. It is impossible to say how much of this absence of growth of productivity is cyclical—and so will be made good as output recovers—and how much it reflects a downward shift in the underlying growth of productivity. There are some grounds for thinking that the large changes in energy prices in 1973 and the low levels of investment in recent years may affect the future growth of productivity. This is an uncertain assumption, but, even allowing for the faster growth of labour supply and the contribution made by the rising output of North Sea oil, in the light of the available evidence it would be imprudent to count on a faster growth of productive potential than 3 per cent a year.

53. The economy, however, has excess capacity, which should permit for a period a rate of growth above that of productive potential. The extent of this slack, and the pace at which it can be taken up, are not easy to determine. The unemployed capacity—both labour and plant—is unevenly distributed, and there are physical constraints on the pace at which manufacturing output can grow without leading to over-heating in some sectors and a sharp worsening of the trade balance. It is essential to aim at a rate of growth that can be sustained over a number of years.

54. That rate of growth will be largely determined by developments in three areas—inflation, productivity and the growth of the world economy. On the last of these, concerted efforts are needed to raise demand and bring down unemployment in the industrialised countries; but the persisting problems of inflation and the OPEC surplus make it unlikely that action taken in the near future will be sufficient to return world trade to the growth rate seen on average in the decade before the oil price rise.

55. In this situation it is more than ever important for British industry to improve its competitiveness both by containing costs and by raising productivity. Only in this way can both high employment and an external current account surplus sufficient for our needs be achieved. Along with a satisfactory balance of payments, the first claim on higher output must be investment. A rise in the proportion of national income devoted to industrial investment is essential both for underpinning a faster growth rate and more generally for increasing industrial efficiency and providing more employment.

12

56. Provided inflation is contained and there is some recovery in world trade, the economy should be able to grow at above its past trend rate. But on present prospects a marked improvement in industrial performance would be necessary to sustain a growth rate above 3½ per cent over the next few years. The aim must be to achieve such an improvement; but it cannot be assumed in advance as a basis for planning public expenditure. With the current degree of unemployment and the bonus of North Sea oil it would be disappointing if a 3½ per cent growth rate were the limit. It should bring down unemployment, but the reduction would be gradual. Even this rate of growth, however, cannot be taken for granted unless inflation is controlled.

57. Table 8 gives projections of the revenue and expenditure, and of the financial balance and borrowing requirement, of general government for the first three years of the survey period. The projections relate to the borrowing requirement of general government (ie central and local government) rather than the more familiar concept of the public sector borrowing requirement, which also includes borrowing by nationalised industries and other public corporations from sources outside government. The definition of public expenditure in these White Papers is now close to that of general government expenditure. The figures in the table are on the basis used by the Central Statistical Office for general government receipts and expenditure, as published in "Financial Statistics".

General government account

TABLE 8   £ billion at 1976–77 prices

	1976–77	1977–78	1978–79	1979–80
Receipts				
1 Taxes on income and expenditure... ...	36·8	36·2	38·2	40·4
2 Capital taxes	0·9	0·8	0·7	0·7
3 National insurance contributions(¹) ...	8·8	8·4	8·0	8·3
4 Other receipts	3·1	3·0	3·1	3·1
5 Interest receipts	2·4	2·6	2·6	2·4
Total receipts	52·0	51·0	52·6	54·9
Expenditure				
1 Expenditure on goods and services ...	32·5	30·2	30·4	31·4
2 Grants and subsidies(²)	19·3	19·7	20·9	20·9
3 Contingency reserve			0·7	1·4
4 Shortfall(³)			−1·0	−1·0
5 Interest payments	5·7	5·8	5·9	5·5
Total expenditure	57·5	55·7	56·9	58·2
Financial balance	−5·5	−4·7	−4·3	−3·3
Net lending and miscellaneous capital receipts, etc	−1·8	−0·8	−1·1	−1·0
General government borrowing requirement(⁴)	−7·3	−5·5	−5·4	−4·3

¹ Includes national health service and redundancy and maternity fund contributions.
² Includes increase in book value of stocks.
³ See paragraph 63.
⁴ Minus sign indicates a borrowing requirement.

13

58. The projections for 1977–78 and 1978–79 are consistent with the forecasts for the public sector borrowing requirement published on 26 October. For 1979–80, they are based on the assumption that GDP will continue to grow at $3\frac{1}{2}$ per cent and that private sector expenditure will be sufficient to produce a level of demand consistent with that growth rate. The figures for 1979–80 are thus not forecasts, but illustrations of what might be consistent with one assumption concerning the growth of GDP.

59. The figures of revenue for 1977–78 and 1978–79 are based on the existing tax rates and the levels of personal allowances announced by the Chancellor of the Exchequer on 26 October. The projections for 1979–80 assume existing tax rates and an increase in personal allowances in line with the forecast rise in retail prices during 1978, following the provisions of the 1977 Finance Act.

60. The figures for public expenditure are based on current programmes, but a number of adjustments have been necessary to make the series consistent with the national accounts concepts used by the CSO. As the table shows the balance of receipts and expenditure, it is necessary also to make some allowance for the likelihood that, for the reasons explained in paragraphs 21–22 above, the outturn of expenditure programmes as a whole will fall somewhat below the planned level. Past experience shows that this kind of underspending varies considerably and cannot be closely predicted for any particular year. For 1977–78, the expenditure figures in this White Paper have already been revised downwards on this account. For 1978–79 and 1979–80, the allowance represents only a very broad judgment about the possible outcome, having regard to the experience of the previous two years, but assuming some improvement in the match between outturn and plans as a result of greater familiarity with the new control and monitoring systems.

61. As with the forecast published on 26 October the projections assume growth of average earnings at 10 per cent a year and an effective exchange rate index of $62\frac{1}{4}$. Both expenditure and revenue are expressed at 1976–77 prices by use of the deflator or for GDP at market prices.

62. Forecasts of borrowing requirements are subject to a wide margin of error. The borrowing requirement is the difference between two large flows, and proportionately small changes in either can be large in relation to the borrowing requirement itself.

63. The projections show total tax revenue (at 1976–77 prices) declining in the current year, reflecting the changes in tax rates and allowances during 1977, but thereafter increasing faster than GDP. An important element in this rise is the growing volume of tax and royalty revenues arising from North Sea oil. These account for approximately £1·4 billion of the £4·1 billion projected rise in tax revenue between 1977–78 and 1979–80. The fall in the real value of social security contributions between 1976–77 and 1977–78 is largely

14

accounted for by the movement of real earnings. The reason for the further fall shown in 1978–79 is that the National Insurance Fund is expected to show an excess of receipts over outgoings this year, but in future years receipts and outgoings are assumed to be roughly in balance.

64. Total general government receipts are projected to rise by about 8 per cent between 1977–78 and 1979–80, and total expenditure by 5 per cent. Thus, at unchanged tax rates, the general government borrowing require-ment, at 1976–77 prices, is projected to fall from about £5½ billion in 1977–78 to about £4½ billion in 1979–80.

Conclusion

65. The public expenditure plans described in this White Paper should permit a sustained improvement in standards, while allowing at the same time a substantial growth in personal consumption after four years of no growth. But this depends on the performance of industry and of the whole economy during the period. There is now, thanks to North Sea oil and to the adjustments achieved in the past year, an opportunity to move to a higher rate of economic growth than has been achieved for many years. But it is only an opportunity. To make it a reality is the major task now facing government, management and unions, and the nation as a whole.

PUBLIC EXPENDITURE BY PROGRAMME AND IN TOTAL

TABLE 9

£ million at 1977 survey prices

	1972–73	1973–74	1974–75	1975–76	1976–77	1977–78	1978–79	1979–80	1980–81	1981–82
1 Defence	6,451	6,370	6,123	6,445	6,361	6,255	6,289	6,494	6,660	6,660
2 Overseas aid and other overseas services	1,185	1,235	1,183	1,008	1,188	1,351	1,722	1,860	1,958	1,962
3 Agriculture, fisheries, food and forestry	881	997	1,950	1,761	1,133	899	706	654	649	642
4 Trade, industry and employment:										
refinance of home shipbuilding and fixed rate export credit	747	874	852	792	636	−174	145	−44	−114	−30
other	2,271	3,267	3,436	2,703	2,542	1,970(¹)	2,798	2,632	2,589	2,547
5 Government lending to nationalised industries	2,085	364	1,116	1,347	330	420	1,350	1,550	1,350	1,100
6 Roads and transport	2,538	2,719	3,079	3,173	2,784	2,590	2,563	2,583	2,572	2,554
7 Housing	3,125	4,127	5,601	4,914	4,870	4,475	4,702	4,814	4,948	4,995
8 Other environmental services	2,705	2,906	2,858	2,926	2,682	2,532	2,594	2,626	2,643	2,657
9 Law, order and protective services	1,532	1,610	1,734	1,851	1,895	1,906	1,948	1,947	1,970	1,992
10 Education and libraries, science and arts	7,674	8,090	8,156	8,319	8,293	8,010	8,102	8,143	8,205	8,255
11 Health and personal social services	6,519	6,863	6,994	7,238	7,287	7,390	7,537	7,652	7,776	7,927
12 Social security	10,675	10,674	11,368	12,309	12,717	13,226	14,063	14,172	14,458	14,602
13 Other public services	985	741	804	888	848	844	854	865	865	886
14 Common services	802	803	800	903	896	883	910	952	986	1,022
15 Northern Ireland	1,402	1,468	1,676	1,725	1,737	1,742	1,815	1,811	1,796	1,808
Total programmes	51,577	53,107	57,729	58,301	56,201	54,320	58,100	58,711	59,310	59,577
Contingency reserve	—	—	—	—	—	—	750	1,500	1,750	2,000
Total	51,577	53,107	57,729	58,301	56,201	54,320	58,850	60,211	61,060	61,577
Debt interest	913	1,082	907	1,169	1,662	1,900	2,000	1,900	1,800	1,600
Total	52,490	54,189	58,636	59,470	57,863	56,220	60,850	62,111	62,860	63,177
Total programmes, contingency reserve and foreign and market borrowing of nationalised industries	51,340	54,501	58,768	59,184	57,635	54,850	58,550	59,611	60,860	61,237

TABLE 10

	1972–73	1973–74	1974–75	1975–76	1976–77	1977–78	1978–79	1979–80	1980–81	1981–82
Current expenditure										
Wages and salaries	15,325	15,932	16,683	17,409	17,642	17,762	18,004	18,142	18,258	18,417
Other current expenditure on goods and services	9,074	9,222	9,389	9,661	9,333	9,411	9,529	9,801	10,088	10,171
Subsidies	2,122	3,624	5,520	4,576	4,098	3,557	3,290	3,115	3,058	3,005
Current grants to persons	11,641	11,641	12,295	13,358	13,888	14,650	15,602	15,795	16,155	16,345
Current grants to private bodies	859	939	995	1,059	1,092	976	1,047	1,053	1,059	1,080
Current grants abroad	487	631	386	552	847	1,034	1,342	1,440	1,556	1,558
Total excluding debt interest	39,508	41,989	45,267	46,615	46,901	47,389	48,812	49,346	50,174	50,576
Capital expenditure										
Gross domestic fixed capital formation	6,472	7,115	6,909	7,014	6,296	5,116	5,363	5,420	5,434	5,462
Increase in value of stocks	130	53	38	68	73	83	88	69	45	45
Capital grants	1,513	1,585	1,442	1,265	1,378	1,485	1,556	1,541	1,546	1,560
Net lending to the private sector	560	735	1,240	484	161	−26	130	153	232	250
Net lending to nationalised industries and some other public corporations(1)	2,129	452	1,230	1,425	552	727	1,737	1,897	1,678	1,418
Net lending to overseas governments	301	236	179	120	96	59	81	74	74	74
Drawings from United Kingdom subscriptions to international lending bodies	66	93	130	157	119	142	167	200	200	200
Other net lending and investment abroad	702	757	762	726	593	−109	150	− 3	− 76	− 11
Cash expenditure on company securities (net)	72	3	333	411	26	−556	3	2	2	2
Capital transfers abroad	126	89	199	16	6	10	13	12	—	—
Total	12,069	11,118	12,462	11,686	9,300	6,931	9,288	9,365	9,135	9,001
Contingency reserve	—	—	—	—	—	—	750	1,500	1,750	2,000
Total	51,577	53,107	57,729	58,301	56,201	54,320	58,850	60,211	61,060	61,577
Debt interest	913	1,082	907	1,169	1,662	1,900	2,000	1,900	1,800	1,600
Total	52,490	54,189	58,636	59,470	57,863	56,220	60,850	62,111	62,860	63,177

1 The principal corporations other than nationalised industries are the National Enterprise Board and the Scottish and Welsh Development Agencies. A list is given in Part 6.

17

TABLE 11   PUBLIC EXPENDITURE BY SPENDING AUTHORITY AND PROGRAMME AND IN TOTAL

£ million at 1977 survey prices

	1972–73	1973–74	1974–75	1975–76	1976–77	1977–78	1978–79	1979–80	1980–81	1981–82
Central government										
Defence and overseas services ...	7,599	7,559	7,272	7,418	7,527	7,589	7,983	8,324	8,589	8,592
Agriculture, fisheries, food and forestry	884	986	1,935	1,747	1,126	892	698	646	641	634
Trade, industry and employment	2,987	4,110	4,254	3,458	3,139	1,748	2,896	2,539	2,426	2,468
Government lending to nationalised industries	2,085	364	1,116	1,347	330	420	1,350	1,550	1,350	1,100
Roads and transport	995	1,134	1,408	1,405	1,186	1,102	1,104	1,092	1,075	1,054
Housing	767	1,082	1,588	1,456	2,066	2,155	2,160	2,120	2,221	2,254
Education and libraries, science and arts	1,310	1,386	1,331	1,355	1,350	1,205	1,254	1,261	1,279	1,305
Health and personal social services	5,695	5,905	5,950	6,124	6,191	6,287	6,406	6,499	6,594	6,712
Social security	10,675	10,674	11,369	12,309	12,717	13,226	14,063	14,172	14,458	14,602
Other programmes including Northern Ireland	3,048	3,045	3,436	3,658	3,605	3,610	3,741	3,775	3,786	3,849
Total programmes	36,046	36,244	39,661	40,279	39,238	38,233	41,655	41,980	42,418	42,570
Local authorities										
Roads and transport	1,542	1,584	1,643	1,731	1,562	1,445	1,428	1,466	1,470	1,472
Housing	2,240	2,838	3,653	3,104	2,524	2,135	2,314	2,416	2,446	2,457
Other environmental services ...	1,864	1,989	2,088	2,140	1,965	1,825	1,888	1,912	1,961	1,974
Law, order and protective services	1,201	1,249	1,330	1,414	1,460	1,459	1,478	1,476	1,488	1,503
Education and libraries, science and arts	6,364	6,703	6,824	6,964	6,942	6,805	6,848	6,882	6,925	6,950
Personal social services ...	824	958	1,044	1,113	1,096	1,103	1,132	1,152	1,183	1,215
Other programmes (Great Britain)	104	122	149	161	148	158	161	165	165	164
Local authorities in Northern Ireland	408	271	200	219	219	234	243	250	252	255
Total programmes	14,546	15,715	16,931	16,846	15,916	15,165	15,493	15,719	15,890	15,992
Certain public corporations(1) ...	985	1,147	1,138	1,176	1,047	922	952	1,012	1,002	1,015
Total programmes	51,577	53,107	57,729	58,301	56,201	54,320	58,100	58,711	59,310	59,577
Contingency reserve	—	—	—	—	—	—	750	1,500	1,750	2,000
Total	51,577	53,107	57,729	58,301	56,201	54,320	58,850	60,211	61,060	61,577
Debt interest	913	1,082	907	1,169	1,662	1,900	2,000	1,900	1,800	1,600
Total	52,490	54,189	58,636	59,470	57,863	56,220	60,850	62,111	62,860	63,177

(1) Corporations whose capital expenditure is included in public...

TABLE 12

£ million at 1977 survey prices

	1972-73	1973-74	1974-75	1975-76	1976-77	1977-78	1978-79	1979-80	1980-81	1981-82
Central government										
Current:										
Goods and services	15,137	15,396	15,659	16,253	16,187	16,381	16,626	16,946	17,261	17,431
Subsidies and grants	14,493	16,058	18,115	18,376	18,789	18,969	20,024	20,103	20,489	20,624
Capital:										
Goods and services	1,682	1,675	1,501	1,648	1,518	1,293	1,450	1,418	1,393	1,415
Grants	1,285	1,281	1,204	1,129	1,247	1,322	1,319	1,293	1,296	1,311
Net lending to nationalised industries and some other public corporations(1)	2,129	452	1,230	1,425	552	727	1,737	1,897	1,678	1,418
Other net lending and capital transactions	1,319	1,384	1,950	1,448	945	−459	499	322	300	371
Total excluding debt interest	36,046	36,244	39,661	40,279	39,238	38,233	41,655	41,980	42,418	42,570
Local authorities										
Current:										
Goods and services	9,262	9,758	10,412	10,817	10,789	10,792	10,907	10,997	11,085	11,157
Subsidies and grants	616	777	1,080	1,169	1,136	1,247	1,255	1,300	1,340	1,364
Capital:										
Goods and services	4,040	4,476	4,498	4,405	3,880	3,016	3,132	3,194	3,220	3,215
Grants	227	302	236	135	128	157	229	240	241	241
Net lending and other capital transactions	402	402	704	321	−16	−47	−30	−11	5	14
Total excluding debt interest	14,546	15,715	16,931	16,846	15,916	15,165	15,493	15,719	15,890	15,992
Certain public corporations(2)										
Capital:										
Goods and services	879	1,017	947	1,030	970	890	869	878	868	877
Grants	1	2	2	3	4	6	8	8	8	8
Net lending and other capital transactions	105	128	189	144	72	26	75	127	126	130
Total	985	1,147	1,138	1,176	1,047	922	952	1,012	1,002	1,015
Total expenditure on programmes	51,577	53,107	57,729	58,301	56,201	54,320	58,100	58,711	59,310	59,577
Contingency reserve	—	—	—	—	—	—	750	1,500	1,750	2,000
Total	51,577	53,107	57,729	58,301	56,201	54,320	58,850	60,211	61,060	61,577
Debt interest	913	1,082	907	1,169	1,662	1,900	2,000	1,900	1,800	1,600
Total	52,490	54,189	58,636	59,470	57,863	56,220	60,850	62,111	62,860	63,177

¹ See note (¹) to table 10.

² See note (¹) to table 11.

19

COMPARISON OF PLANNED EXPENDITURE AND ESTIMATED OUT-TURN IN 1976–77 and 1977–78 BY SPENDING AUTHORITY AND ECONOMIC CATEGORY

TABLE 13 £ million at 1977 survey prices

	1976–77		1977–78	
	Difference	Percentage change	Difference	Percentage change
Central government				
Current:				
Goods and services	−560	− 3·3	−146	− 0·9
Subsidies and grants	−317	− 1·7	+ 32	+ 0·2
Capital:				
Goods and services	− 23	− 1·5	− 65	− 4·8
Grants...	− 71	− 5·4	+130	+ 10·9
Net lending to nationalised industries and some other public corporations(¹) ...	−659	− 54·4	−508	− 41·1
Other net lending and capital transactions	−168	− 15·2	−782	...
Total	−1,798	− 4·4	−1,339	− 3·4
Local authorities				
Current:				
Goods and services	−274	− 2·5	−110	− 1·0
Subsidies and grants	− 46	− 3·9	− 84	− 6·3
Capital:				
Goods and services	− 62	− 1·6	− 93	− 3·0
Grants...	− 58	− 31·2	− 20	− 11·3
Net lending and other capital transactions	− 62	—	+ 65	...
Total	−502	− 3·1	−242	− 1·6
Certain public corporations(²)				
Capital:				
Goods and services	−101	− 9·4	− 37	− 4·0
Grants...	—	—	—	—
Net lending and other capital transactions	− 3	− 3·9	− 34	− 56·7
Total	−104	− 9·0	− 71	− 7·2
Total expenditure on programmes	−2,404	− 4·1	−1,652	− 3·0
Contingency reserve			−750	
Total			−2,402	− 4·2

¹ See note (¹) to table 10.
² See note (¹) to table 11.

SUMMARY OF CHANGES SINCE CMND 6721

£ million at 1977 survey prices

	Pro-gramme(1)	1976–77	1977–78	1978–79	1979–80	1980–81
March 1977 Budget measures						
Employment schemes(2) ...	4		+63	+66	+6	+4
Inner cities (construction) ...	8		+14	+74	—	—
Effect of tax changes on child benefit tax offset	12		+4	+4	+4	+4
			+81	+144	+10	+8
Statement of 25 May 1977						
1977 uprating of social security benefits	12		+46	+120	+120	+120
Statement of 29 June 1977						
Employment measures ...	4		+6	+131	+200	+198
Associated education expenditure	10		—	+4	+12	+18
			+6	+135	+212	+216
Statement of 15 July 1977						
Milk subsidy	3		+115	—	—	—
Electricity discount scheme ...	4		+19	+3	—	—
Additional assistance to industry	4		+4	+14	+16	+9
Extension of eligibility for free school meals	10		+17	+30	+32	+29
Child benefit	12		+7	+314	+308	+302
Construction	various		+93	—	—	—
			+255	+361	+356	+340
Statement of 26 October 1977						
Construction	various		—	+369	+200	—
Overseas aid	2		—	+20	—	—
Assistance to small firms ...	4		—	+2	—	—
Law and order	9		—	+10	+11	+11
Education, science and arts ...	10		—	+10	+10	+10
Health authorities	11		—	+12	+12	+12
Local authorities, personal social services	11		—	+6	+6	+6
Christmas bonus for pensioners	12		+97	—	—	—
Uprating of mobility allowance	12		—	+14	+18	+19
Effect of tax changes on child benefit tax offset	12		+3	+14	+14	+14
			+100	+457	+271	+72
Other announced changes ...	various	+7	+225	+165	+155	+137
Other changes	various	−2,411	−2,365	+232	−34(3)	+937(3)
Total changes to programmes ...		−2,404	−1,652	+1,614	+1,090(3)	+1,830(3)
Change to contingency reserve		—	−750	−275		
Total change		−2,404	−2,402	+1,339		
Change to debt interest ...		−98	−600	−500		
Change to total public expenditure		−2,502	−3,002	+839		
Total change to programmes, contingency reserve and net overseas and market borrowing of nationalised industries ...		−1,988	−2,412	+970		

(1) In addition to the programmes shown, many of these changes affect expenditure on programme 15—orthern Ireland.
(2) Includes employment package announced on 3 March.
(3) Excludes refinancing of home shipbuilding lending and fixed rate export credits, government lending to tionalised industries and debt interest for which no estimates were published in Cmnd 6721.

CHANGES TO EXPENDITURE PROGRAMMES SINCE CMND 6721

TABLE 15 £ million at 1977 survey pri

	1976–77	1977–78	1978–79	1979–80(¹)	1980–81
1. Defence					
Statement of 26 October: construction	—	—	+8	—	—
Other changes	−170	−71	+4	−50	+122
	−170	−71	+12	−50	+122
2. Overseas aid and other overseas services					
Statement of 26 October	—	—	+20	—	—
Butter subsidy—EEC contribution (27 April)	—	−51	−2	—	—
Other changes(²)	−108	−117	+29	−16	+28
	−108	−168	+47	−16	+28
3. Agriculture, fisheries, food and forestry					
Statement of 15 July: milk subsidy	—	+115	—	—	—
Other announced changes:					
Pig subsidy (20 January)	+6	+10	—	—	—
Private woodland grants (30 March)	—	—	+1	+1	+2
Butter subsidy (27 April)	—	+68	+1	—	—
Potato support (5 October)	—	+3	+2	—	—
Milk subsidy (9 December)	—	+23	—	—	—
Agricultural capital grants (16 December)	—	+10	+5	+2	+2
Other changes(²)	−22	+55	+119	+81	+76
	−16	+284	+128	+84	+80
4. Trade, industry and employment					
March 1977 Budget measures: employment schemes(³)	—	+63	+66	+6	+4
Statement of 29 June: employment measures	—	+6	+131	+200	+198
Statement of 15 July:					
Electricity discount scheme	—	+19	+3	—	—
Additional assistance to industry(⁴)	—	+4	+14	+16	+9
Statement of 26 October:					
Construction	—	—	+18	+8	—
Assistance to small firms	—	—	+2	—	—
Other announced changes:					
Marathon: assistance with rig (22 December 1976)	—	+6	—	−1	−1
Redundancy Rebates Bill (7 February)	—	+9	+2	+2	+2
Support for shipbuilding industry (24 February)	—	—	+14	+8	—
Coal for Scottish power stations (12 March)	—	+7	+7	+7	+7
Regrading assisted areas (14 April)	—	+1	+5	—	—
Kirkby Manufacturing and Engineering Ltd (26 April)	—	+1	—	—	—
Rephasing of grants to Govan Shipbuilders (29 June)	—	+2	—	—	—
Extension of Price Commission powers (22 July)	—	+2	+4	+4	+4
Instrumentation and automation industry scheme (9 August)	—	—	+1	+2	+2
Drop forging industry scheme (8 November)	—	—	—	+1	+1
Energy conservation (12 December)	—	—	+3	+7	+9
Regional development grants (16 December)	—	+78	+20	—	—
Other changes:					
Refinancing of home shipbuilding lending and fixed rate export credits	−57	−577	−237	...	...
Other	−375	−336	+20	+108(⁵)	+112
	−432	−715	+73	+368(⁵)	+347

22

£ million at 1977 survey prices

	1976–77	1977–78	1978–79	1979–80(¹)	1980–81(¹)
Government lending to nationalised industries	−587	−440	+319	...(⁶)	...(⁶)
Roads and transport					
Statement of 15 July: construction ...	—	+4	—	—	—
Statement of 26 October: construction ...	—	—	+28	+12	—
Other announced changes:					
Airport security (18 February)	—	—	−9	−11	−11
IMCO building (26 October)	—	+4	+8	+7	+2
Other changes	−273	−104	+39	+27	+47
	−273	−96	+66	+35	+38
Housing					
Statement of 15 July: construction ...	—	+47	—	—	—
Statement of 16 October: construction ...	—	—	+172	+103	—
Other announced changes:					
Housing improvements (2 May) ...	—	+30	—	—	—
Local authority mortgage lending etc, Wales (20 June)	—	+2	—	—	—
Local authority mortgage lending etc, Scotland (30 June)	—	+5	—	—	—
National housing survey (6 July) ...	—	+1	+1	—	—
Additions offset by reductions in housing subsidies etc	—	−38	−1	—	—
Energy conservation (12 December) ...	—	—	+11	+19	+20
Other changes	−284	−311	−206	−401(⁷)	−166(⁷)
	−284	−264	−23	−279(⁷)	−146(⁷)
Other environmental services					
March 1977 Budget measures: inner cities construction	—	+14	+74	—	—
Statement of 15 July: construction ...	—	+15	—	—	—
Statement of 26 October: construction ...	—	—	+49	+27	—
Other changes	−166	−42	+21	−133	−73
	−166	−13	+144	−106	−73
Law, order and protective services					
Statement of 26 October:					
Law and order measures	—	—	+10	+11	+11
Construction	—	—	+9	+5	—
Other changes	−38	−11	+39	+30	+59
	−38	−11	+58	+46	+70
Education and libraries, science and arts					
Statement of 29 June: Holland report—associated education expenditure ...	—	—	+4	+12	+18
Statement of 15 July:					
Extension of eligibility for free school meals	—	+17	+30	+32	+29
Construction	—	+12	—	—	—
Statement of 26 October:					
Teachers, discretionary awards, science and arts	—	—	+10	+10	+10
Construction	—	—	+31	+16	—
Energy conservation (12 December) ...	—	—	+5	+14	+12
Other changes	−76	−156	+11	+37	+76
	−76	−127	+90	+121	+145

TABLE 15—continued £ million at 1977 survey pric

	1976–77	1977–78	1978–79	1979–80(¹)	1980–81
11. Health and personal social services					
Statement of 15 July: construction	—	+15	—	—	—
Statement of 26 October:					
Health authorities	—	—	+12	+12	+12
Local authorities' personal social services	—	—	+6	+6	+6
Construction	—	—	+40	+20	—
Other announced changes:					
Withdrawal of NHS road traffic accidents charges scheme (14 February)	—	+21	+45	+45	+45
Energy conservation (12 December)	—	—	+2	+6	+2
Other changes	−72	−1	+6	—	+142
	−72	+35	+111	+89	+207
12. Social security					
March 1977 Budget measures:					
Effect of tax changes on child benefit tax offset	—	+4	+4	+4	+4
Statement of 25 May: 1977 uprating of benefits	—	+46	+120	+120	+120
Statement of 15 July: child benefit	—	+7	+314	+308	+302
Statement of 26 October:					
Christmas bonus for pensioners	—	−97	—	—	—
Uprating of mobility allowance ...	—	—	+14	+18	+19
Effect of tax changes on child benefit tax offset	—	+3	+14	+14	+14
Other announced changes:					
Miscellaneous Provisions Bill (22 March)	—	+11	+15	+15	+15
Other changes	−9	−222	+13	+244	+456
	−9	−54	+494	+723	+930
13. Other public services					
Statement of 26 October: construction	—	—	+2	—	—
Other changes	−33	−15	—	+4	+2
	−33	−15	+2	+4	+2
14. Common services					
Statement of 26 October: construction	—	—	+3	+4	—
Other changes	−43	+11	+22	+8	+19
	−43	+11	+25	+12	+19
15. Northern Ireland					
Announced changes: consequentials of changes to GB programmes	+1	+20	+34	+32	+24
Other changes	−98	−28	+34	+27	+37
	−97	−8	+68	+59	+61
Total changes to programmes	−2,404	−1,652	+1,614	+1,090(⁸)	+1,830

(¹) Cmnd 6721—I, paragraph 4, explained that the figures for 1979–80 and 1980–81 were even mc provisional than usual, since they had not been further reviewed in the light of the developments which ha led to the reductions in programmes for 1977–78 and 1978–79 announced on 15 December 1976. The chang for these years in this White Paper need to be read with this in mind.

(²) Mainly increased expenditure on market regulation under the common agricultural policy, partly off by increased receipts from the EEC.

(³) Includes employment package announced on 3 March.

(⁴) Product and process development scheme and additional allocations for the ferrous foundries a machine tools industry schemes.

(⁵) Excludes refinancing of home shipbuilding lending and fixed rate export credits for which comparal estimates were not published in Cmnd 6721.

(⁶) No comparable estimates published in Cmnd 6721.

(⁷) These changes are mainly due to revisions in the figures for housing subsidies in the light of rece changes in interest rates; the figures for subsidies, and the overall size of the programme, must be to sor extent provisional (see part 2, chapter 7, paragraphs 4 and 5).

(⁸) See footnote (³) to table 14.

CHANGES TO EXPENDITURE PROGRAMMES SINCE CMND 6721 BY ECONOMIC CATEGORY

£ million at 1977 survey prices

	1976–77	1977–78	1978–79	1979–80	1980–81
March 1977 Budget measures					
Current: goods and services	—	+4	+3	—	—
subsidies and grants	—	+63	+67	+10	+8
Capital: goods and services	—	+14	+74	—	—
	—	+81	+144	+10	+8
Statement of 25 May 1977					
Current: subsidies and grants	—	+46	+120	+120	+120
Statement of 29 June 1977					
Current: goods and services	—	+1	+7	+14	+17
subsidies and grants	—	+5	+127	+193	+191
Capital: goods and services	—	—	+1	+5	+8
	—	+6	+135	+212	+216
Statement of 15 July 1977					
Current: goods and services	—	+18	+30	+32	+29
subsidies and grants	—	+142	+317	+308	+302
Capital: goods and services	—	+51	—	—	—
grants	—	+24	+14	+16	+9
net lending and other capital transactions	—	+20	—	—	—
	—	+255	+361	+356	+340
Statement of 26 October 1977					
Current: goods and services	—	—	+42	+26	+23
subsidies and grants	—	+100	+69	+54	+48
Capital: goods and services	—	—	+332	+189	+1
grants	—	—	+14	+2	—
	—	+100	+457	+271	+72
Other announced changes					
Current: goods and services	—	+26	+57	+65	+66
subsidies and grants	+7	+57	+60	+47	+46
Capital: goods and services	—	+34	+7	+27	+24
grants	—	+95	+34	+15	+6
net lending and other capital transactions	—	+13	+7	+1	−5
	+7	+225	+165	+155	+137
Other changes					
Current: goods and services	−834	−305	+5	−1	+379
subsidies and grants	−370	−465	+108	+331	+585
Capital: goods and services	−186	−294	+10	−362	−134
grants	−129	−9	+56	−41	−35
net lending to nationalised industries and some other public corporations	−659	−508	+319	+43	+50
other net lending and capital transactions	−233	−784	−266	−4	+92
	−2,411	−2,365	+232	−34(1)	+937(1)

25

TABLE 16—continued   £ million at 1977 survey prices

		1976–77	1977–78	1978–79	1979–80	1980–81
H.	**Summary of changes**					
Current:	goods and services	−834	−256	+144	+136	+514
	subsidies and grants	−363	−52	+868	+1,063	+1,300
Capital:	goods and services	−186	−195	+424	−141	−101
	grants	−129	+110	+118	−8	−20
	net lending to nationalised industries and some other public corporations	−659	−508	+319	+43	+50
	other net lending and capital transactions	−233	−751	−259	−3	+87
		−2,404	−1,652	+1,614	+1,090(1)	+1,830

(¹) See footnote (³) to table 14.

Printed in England for Her Majesty's Stationery Office by Oyez Press Limited
Dd291026   D60   K88   12/77